Everything You Ever Wanted to Know About Cincinnati Bengals

Everything You Ever Wanted to Know About….

Absolutely nothing, because we really don't care…

Everything You Ever Wanted to Know About...

Absolutely nothing, because we really don't care...

Everything You Ever Wanted to Know About...

Absolutely nothing, because we really don't care...

Everything You Ever Wanted to Know About...

Absolutely nothing, because we really don't care...

Everything You Ever Wanted to Know About…

Absolutely nothing, because we really don't care…

Everything You Ever Wanted to Know About...

Absolutely nothing, because we really don't care...

Everything You Ever Wanted to Know About...

Absolutely nothing, because we really don't care...

Everything You Ever Wanted to Know About...

Absolutely nothing, because we really don't care...

Everything You Ever Wanted to Know About…

Absolutely nothing, because we really don't care…

Everything You Ever Wanted to Know About...

Absolutely nothing, because we really don't care...

Everything You Ever Wanted to Know About…

Absolutely nothing, because we really don't care…

Everything You Ever Wanted to Know About...

Absolutely nothing, because we really don't care....

Everything You Ever Wanted to Know About....

Absolutely nothing, because we really don't care...

Everything You Ever Wanted to Know About...

Absolutely nothing, because we really don't care.....

Everything You Ever Wanted to Know About.....

Absolutely nothing, because we really don't care...

Everything You Ever Wanted to Know About...

Absolutely nothing, because we really don't care...

Everything You Ever Wanted to Know About...

Absolutely nothing, because we really don't care...

Everything You Ever Wanted to Know About...

Absolutely nothing, because we really don't care...

Everything You Ever Wanted to Know About...

Absolutely nothing, because we really don't care...

Everything You Ever Wanted to Know About...

Absolutely nothing, because we really don't care...

Everything You Ever Wanted to Know About...

Absolutely nothing, because we really don't care...

Everything You Ever Wanted to Know About...

Absolutely nothing, because we really don't care...

Everything You Ever Wanted to Know About...

Absolutely nothing, because we really don't care...

Everything You Ever Wanted to Know About…

Absolutely nothing, because we really don't care…

Everything You Ever Wanted to Know About…

Absolutely nothing, because we really don't care…

Everything You Ever Wanted to Know About...

Absolutely nothing, because we really don't care...

Everything You Ever Wanted to Know About...

Absolutely nothing, because we really don't care...

Everything You Ever Wanted to Know About...

Absolutely nothing, because we really don't care...

Everything You Ever Wanted to Know About...

Absolutely nothing, because we really don't care...

Everything You Ever Wanted to Know About...

Absolutely nothing, because we really don't care...

Everything You Ever Wanted to Know About...

Absolutely nothing, because we really don't care...

Everything You Ever Wanted to Know About…

Absolutely nothing, because we really don't care…

Everything You Ever Wanted to Know About...

Absolutely nothing, because we really don't care...

Everything You Ever Wanted to Know About...

Absolutely nothing, because we really don't care....

Everything You Ever Wanted to Know About....

Absolutely nothing, because we really don't care...

Everything You Ever Wanted to Know About...

Absolutely nothing, because we really don't care...

Everything You Ever Wanted to Know About...

Absolutely nothing, because we really don't care...

Everything You Ever Wanted to Know About...

Absolutely nothing, because we really don't care...

Everything You Ever Wanted to Know About…

Absolutely nothing, because we really don't care…

Everything You Ever Wanted to Know About....

Absolutely nothing, because we really don't care...

Everything You Ever Wanted to Know About....

Absolutely nothing, because we really don't care...

Everything You Ever Wanted to Know About...

Absolutely nothing, because we really don't care...

Everything You Ever Wanted to Know About...

Absolutely nothing, because we really don't care...

Everything You Ever Wanted to Know About...

Absolutely nothing, because we really don't care...

Everything You Ever Wanted to Know About...

Absolutely nothing, because we really don't care...

Everything You Ever Wanted to Know About...

Absolutely nothing, because we really don't care.....

Absolutely nothing, because we really don't care...

Everything You Ever Wanted to Know About...

Absolutely nothing, because we really don't care...

Everything You Ever Wanted to Know About...

Absolutely nothing, because we really don't care...

Everything You Ever Wanted to Know About...

Absolutely nothing, because we really don't care...

Absolutely nothing, because we really don't care...

Everything You Ever Wanted to Know About...

Absolutely nothing, because we really don't care...

Everything You Ever Wanted to Know About...

Absolutely nothing, because we really don't care...

Everything You Ever Wanted to Know About...

Absolutely nothing, because we really don't care...

Absolutely nothing, because we really don't care...

Everything You Ever Wanted to Know About...

Absolutely nothing, because we really don't care...

Everything You Ever Wanted to Know About...

Absolutely nothing, because we really don't care...

Everything You Ever Wanted to Know About...

Absolutely nothing, because we really don't care....

Everything You Ever Wanted to Know About.....

Absolutely nothing, because we really don't care...

Everything You Ever Wanted to Know About...

Absolutely nothing, because we really don't care...

Everything You Ever Wanted to Know About...

Absolutely nothing, because we really don't care....

Everything You Ever Wanted to Know About...

Absolutely nothing, because we really don't care...

Everything You Ever Wanted to Know About...

Absolutely nothing, because we really don't care...

Everything You Ever Wanted to Know About...

Absolutely nothing, because we really don't care...

Everything You Ever Wanted to Know About...

Absolutely nothing, because we really don't care...

Everything You Ever Wanted to Know About...

Absolutely nothing, because we really don't care....

Everything You Ever Wanted to Know About....

Absolutely nothing, because we really don't care...

Everything You Ever Wanted to Know About...

Absolutely nothing, because we really don't care...

Everything You Ever Wanted to Know About…

Absolutely nothing, because we really don't care…

Everything You Ever Wanted to Know About...

Absolutely nothing, because we really don't care...

Everything You Ever Wanted to Know About...

Absolutely nothing, because we really don't care...

Everything You Ever Wanted to Know About...

Absolutely nothing, because we really don't care...

Absolutely nothing, because we really don't care...

Everything You Ever Wanted to Know About...

Absolutely nothing, because we really don't care...

Absolutely nothing, because we really don't care......

Everything You Ever Wanted to Know About...

Absolutely nothing, because we really don't care...

Everything You Ever Wanted to Know About...

Absolutely nothing, because we really don't care...

Everything You Ever Wanted to Know About...

Absolutely nothing, because we really don't care....

Everything You Ever Wanted to Know About...

Absolutely nothing, because we really don't care...

Everything You Ever Wanted to Know About...

Absolutely nothing, because we really don't care...

Everything You Ever Wanted to Know About...

Absolutely nothing, because we really don't care...

Everything You Ever Wanted to Know About...

Absolutely nothing, because we really don't care...

Everything You Ever Wanted to Know About...

Absolutely nothing, because we really don't care...

Everything You Ever Wanted to Know About...

Absolutely nothing, because we really don't care...

Everything You Ever Wanted to Know About...

Absolutely nothing, because we really don't care...

Absolutely nothing, because we really don't care...

Everything You Ever Wanted to Know About...

Absolutely nothing, because we really don't care...

Everything You Ever Wanted to Know About...

Absolutely nothing, because we really don't care...

Everything You Ever Wanted to Know About...

Absolutely nothing, because we really don't care...

Absolutely nothing, because we really don't care....

Everything You Ever Wanted to Know About....

Absolutely nothing, because we really don't care...

Everything You Ever Wanted to Know About...

Absolutely nothing, because we really don't care...

Everything You Ever Wanted to Know About…

Absolutely nothing, because we really don't care…

Everything You Ever Wanted to Know About...

Absolutely nothing, because we really don't care...

Everything You Ever Wanted to Know About...

Absolutely nothing, because we really don't care...

Everything You Ever Wanted to Know About...

Absolutely nothing, because we really don't care...

Everything You Ever Wanted to Know About...

Absolutely nothing, because we really don't care...

Everything You Ever Wanted to Know About...

Absolutely nothing, because we really don't care...

Everything You Ever Wanted to Know About...

Absolutely nothing, because we really don't care...

Everything You Ever Wanted to Know About...

Absolutely nothing, because we really don't care...

Absolutely nothing, because we really don't care...

Everything You Ever Wanted to Know About...

Absolutely nothing, because we really don't care...

Everything You Ever Wanted to Know About...

Absolutely nothing, because we really don't care...

Everything You Ever Wanted to Know About...

Absolutely nothing, because we really don't care...

Everything You Ever Wanted to Know About...

Absolutely nothing, because we really don't care...

Everything You Ever Wanted to Know About...

Absolutely nothing, because we really don't care...

Absolutely nothing, because we really don't care...

Everything You Ever Wanted to Know About...

Absolutely nothing, because we really don't care...

Everything You Ever Wanted to Know About...

Absolutely nothing, because we really don't care...

Everything You Ever Wanted to Know About...

Absolutely nothing, because we really don't care...

Everything You Ever Wanted to Know About...

Absolutely nothing, because we really don't care...

Everything You Ever Wanted to Know About...

Absolutely nothing, because we really don't care...

Everything You Ever Wanted to Know About...

Absolutely nothing, because we really don't care...

Everything You Ever Wanted to Know About...

Absolutely nothing, because we really don't care...

Everything You Ever Wanted to Know About...

Absolutely nothing, because we really don't care...

Everything You Ever Wanted to Know About…

Absolutely nothing, because we really don't care…

Everything You Ever Wanted to Know About...

Absolutely nothing, because we really don't care...

Everything You Ever Wanted to Know About...

Absolutely nothing, because we really don't care...

Everything You Ever Wanted to Know About...

Absolutely nothing, because we really don't care...

Everything You Ever Wanted to Know About....

Absolutely nothing, because we really don't care...

Everything You Ever Wanted to Know About...

Absolutely nothing, because we really don't care.....

Everything You Ever Wanted to Know About...

Absolutely nothing, because we really don't care...

Everything You Ever Wanted to Know About…

Absolutely nothing, because we really don't care…

Everything You Ever Wanted to Know About...

Absolutely nothing, because we really don't care...

Everything You Ever Wanted to Know About…

Absolutely nothing, because we really don't care…

Everything You Ever Wanted to Know About...

Absolutely nothing, because we really don't care...

Everything You Ever Wanted to Know About...

Absolutely nothing, because we really don't care...

Everything You Ever Wanted to Know About...

Absolutely nothing, because we really don't care...

Everything You Ever Wanted to Know About...

Absolutely nothing, because we really don't care...

Absolutely nothing at all, because we really don’t care...

Made in United States
North Haven, CT
11 October 2022

25315410R00075